BIBLE FAMILIES
Martha and Mary

Linda and Alan Parry

AUGSBURG
MINNEAPOLIS, USA

HUNT & THORPE
ALTON, UNITED KINGDOM

Martha and Mary were sisters, and lived together.

'Hurray!' they shouted. 'Jesus is coming.'

‘I can’t wait to hear what Jesus says,’ Mary said.

'They'll be hungry when they arrive,' said Martha. 'I'll start getting supper.'

‘I’m going to meet them,’ called Mary, already half way down the road.
‘Aren’t you going to help me get things ready?’ asked Martha. But Mary had gone.

'I'd better start sweeping,' thought Martha.
'And then there's the washing. And the cleaning.'

By the time Jesus and his friends arrived,
Martha was almost too busy to say hello!

‘Oh, no! There are more than I thought. Is there enough to drink? Oops! The pot’s boiling over. Is there time to get some more

meat? I wonder how long they're going to stay!' thought Martha.

Meanwhile Mary made everyone comfortable. She kept the best place for herself – down by Jesus' feet.

'I want to hear every word you say,' she told Jesus.

Martha could hear Jesus teaching in the next room. ‘Sounds interesting,’ she thought. ‘But food comes first.’

The busier she got, the angrier she became. 'Why should it always be me who does the work?' she thought. 'It's not fair. I need a rest too.'

Finally Martha stormed into the next room.

‘Lord, can’t you see that I’m doing all this work on my own?’ she complained. ‘Order Mary to help me.’

'Martha, Martha,' Jesus said. 'Mary has chosen to listen to my words – and that is

more important than anything else.'

Martha soon calmed down, and Mary made room for her at Jesus' feet. Martha understood that Jesus was right – to listen to Him was more important than anything.
And afterward they all helped with the washing up!

You can read this story in the Bible
in Luke 10:38-42.

First published by **Hunt & Thorpe** in the United Kingdom, 1990
ISBN 1 85608 075 7
and by **Augsburg** in North America, 1990
ISBN 0-8066-2487-6, LCCN 90-80558
The CIP catalogue record for this book is available from the British Library.

Manufactured in Great Britain.